it could happen to you

A K Dolven

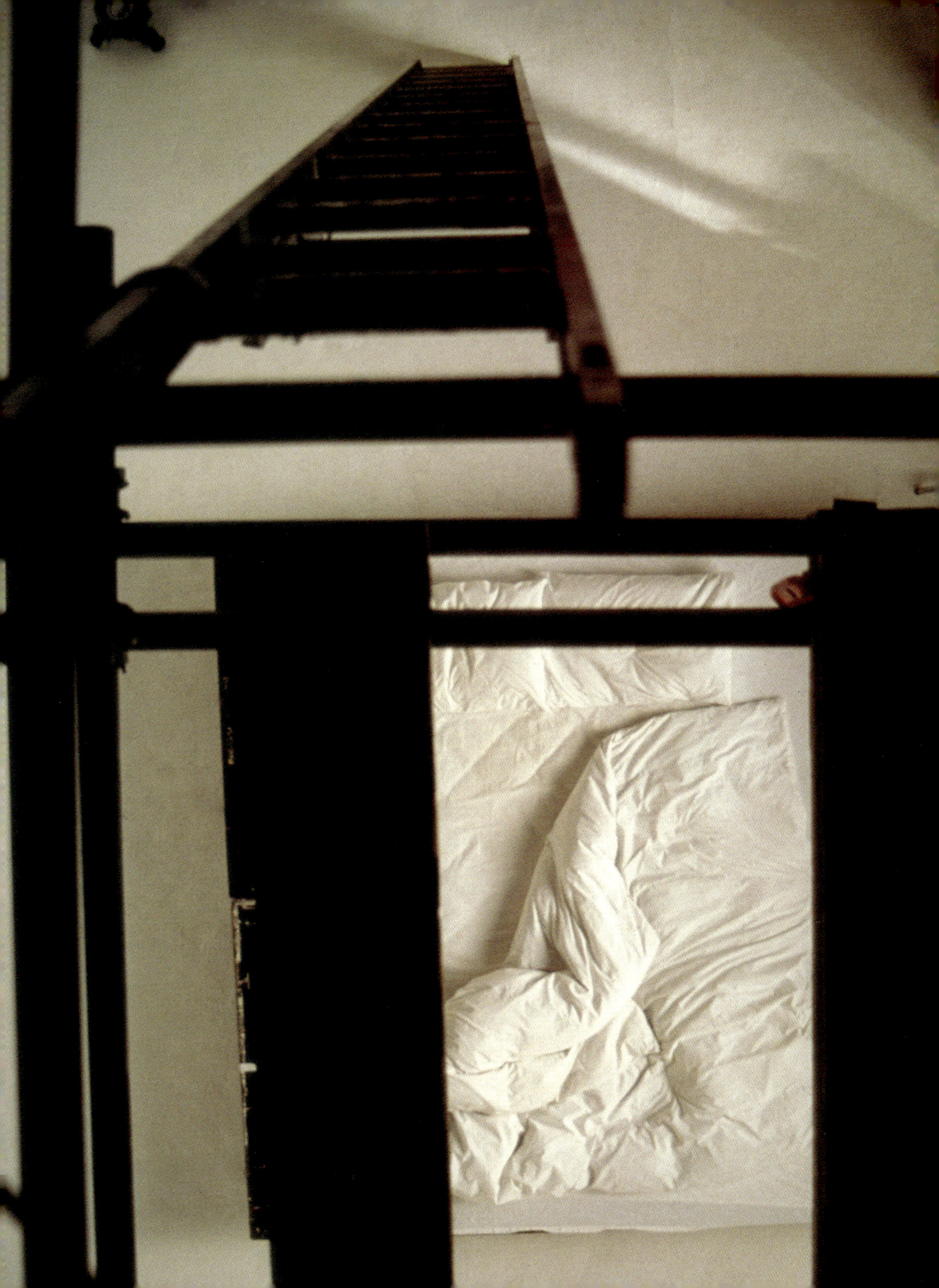

Anne Katrine Dolven
Steven Bode

The Norwegian artist Anne Katrine Dolven has only been exhibiting her film and video works for a little over four years but in that time has attracted considerable attention for her coolly composed and evocative imagery (Dolven began and still works as a painter) and for the fresh twist these videos bring to classical forms like the landscape and the still life. A recent series of video portraits, based on paintings by Norway's early-modernist master Edvard Munch, exerts an equal fascination — not least because of Munch's exalted standing, not just in Norway but within a wider art-historical pantheon. Dolven is acutely aware of this, of course, and her treatment of these canonical works inclines as much towards *hommage* as deconstruction. In each of her five separate video pieces, Dolven sticks respectfully close to the outline of the original - replicating its play of colour, emulating its framing and composition - while introducing new visual elements that provide a more contemporary resonance.

The video 'puberty' (2000) typifies Dolven's approach. The painting it draws from, dating from 1894, is one of Munch's most enduring images, a compelling study of a naked adolescent girl, poised uncomfortably between childish innocence and rapidly-approaching womanhood. In Dolven's video, Munch's gauche and fretful sitter, pinned like a butterfly at the edge of her bed, tremulous at the onset of sexual awakening, is reincarnated in the guise of a modern teenager listening to music on her Walkman in her bedroom. She, too, is naked, and adopts an identical pose, yet there is a world of difference in demeanour and attitude. Though the fact that we are now observing her on video might be expected to heighten the sense of voyeurism and intrusion, the time we spend with her - watching her absent-mindedly drumming her finger, noting her easy confidence in her nakedness - restores a self-possession that is absent from the startled figure in the painting, and lends a warmth and a humanity to an image which, over the intervening hundred years, has, in truth, become something of a cipher.

Munch's 'Self Portrait with Cigarette' (1895) is a comparatively lesser-known work, although half-familiar as a representative example of a particular sub-genre of portrait painting that was highly popular at the turn of the century. Shrouded in smoke, self-assertive and a little self-important, Munch contemplates his art work - himself - with quiet satisfaction. In her video, 'portrait with cigarette' (2000), Dolven interposes another young woman, whose sullen stare at the camera barely relents in the six minutes (and eighteen seconds) that it takes for her cigarette to burn down to ash. She radiates nothing of the cocksure composure of her artist-mentor, and spends the time fidgeting with her remote-control handset, switching channels or cranking up the volume, as she looks for something to distract her, or to hold her attention. Dolven's use of the element of time deftly captures the restless spirit of her subject – a world away from the Romantic vision of the self that is exhibited in the painting, and the total opposite of her counterpart in 'puberty'.

'The Kiss' (1897) is one of Munch's most celebrated paintings: an unforgettable image of two lovers dissolving into one another; a vivid emblem of the thrilling (and sometimes threatening) loss-of-self that is forged in the heat of sexual desire. In her film, 'The Kiss' (2000), Dolven shoots a young couple in the selfsame clinch, and sets their avid, slowburning embrace to the steady throb of a nightclub beat. The flaring, over-exposed colours, while echoing the red motif of the painting, induce a kind of chemically-altered mood, heightened by the insistent, repeating patterns of the trance-like House music. Throughout all this, the figures hardly move, so wrapped up are they in each other. One supposes that this must be love – or at least the impassioned, romantic ecstacy of Munch's first kiss. Then again, judging by the small-hours warehouse setting, the blurring of bodily boundaries might just as easily be the product of ecstacy's chemical derivative.

'it could happen to you' (2001) alludes, in part, to another iconic Munch painting, 'The Sick Child' (1896). Here, too, Dolven reverses the symbolism of the original, raising Munch's red-haired girl from her sick-bed and placing her at the side of an apparently ailing older man. A complex study in nuance and ambivalence, 'it could happen to you' stands apart from the other video portraits (and from much of the rest of Dolven's work) in the way that its preoccupation with significant details invites a wider narrative reading. 'portrait with cigarette', 'puberty', and 'The Kiss' all have the unchanging stature of tableaux, fixed on a moment when time (whether through boredom, bliss or self-absorption) gives the impression of standing still. In 'it could happen to you', time, whilst not exactly racing, moves forward inexorably toward some kind of immanent denouement.

'it could happen to you' is a micro-drama in four acts. A man and a (younger) woman lie on a bed – he, under the covers; she, with her tousled flame of hair and her fashionable boots and clothes, on top of the plain, white sheets. Her actions towards him seem tender and consoling; what's less clear is whether she is ministering to him in illness, or attempting to soften an emotional hurt that she might herself have caused. (The sight of her high-heeled boots against the bed-cover, while asserting her impetuous bohemian spirit, suggests that her presence here may be only temporary.) Her overtures meet with little response — although whether this is because the man is at the end of his strength or the limit of his patience is hard to tell: the moment when she reaches for his hand, only for it to fall, limply, from her grasp, can be read in either way.

The complexion of the whole scene changes, however, when the man, summoning his energy or swallowing his pride, twists across the pillow, and, in an image of ghastly vulnerability, searches for her blindly with his mouth. It is her turn now to fail to reciprocate — instead, she lowers her head, so that his lips brush lightly across her hair. Is she rebuffing him, or is it more that she is simply unable to cope with the anguish of these dying moments? The film's final twist, when she runs a finger provocatively over his mouth, only heightens this underlying *frisson* of ambiguity. As she withdraws her finger with a vampish flourish, is she making it clear that she is cruelly dismissing him, or leaving him with an image of a sexual heat that is no longer possible for the two of them to rekindle? Which do we want it to be: death scene or love scene? Even after several repeat plays, there is no definitive answer; only further confirmation that the intimacies of love and the sorrows of loss are profoundly and inextricably linked.

In the gallery, the piece unfolds in a narrow, self-contained room, with the other video portraits occupying their own discrete spaces. Just as the murmur of traffic, and the muted thud of nearby music, intrude on the intensely private affair, these other personae lurk at its margins, adding their own subtle inflections (is the girl with the cigarette a jealous antagonist?; who exactly are the lovers sharing the passionate kiss?) or simply connecting this highly personal but everyday drama with the endless cycle of human events. A girl retreats to her own secret universe; another is bored to distraction; two people kiss as if they want that moment never to end. Life goes on: oblivious, indifferent.

Such speculative connections are further encouraged by a new piece, 'Headlights' (2001), which, again, has its origins in Munch, in the form of a wood-cut called 'Into the Forest'. It is night, and a car has been parked at the side of an isolated road, its headlights scything a path through the darkness towards the outline of a nearby wood. A man and a woman (the man clothed, the woman naked) stand full-square in the beam of light, then walk off together, in serene but sinister lockstep, before disappearing into the void. The piece has the haunting, indelible imprint of a dream-image, simultaneously arousing and disturbing.

The penetrating glare of the headlights evokes the strange phallic moonglow that looms in the background of a number of paintings such as 'The Voice' (1893) and 'Moonlight' (1895), while the pale gleam of the woman's body, visible long after the man's has vanished, suggests a devouring vampiric sexuality that all-too-regularly surfaces in Munch's representations of women. Once again, we are left to ponder its relation to the protagonists of Dolven's other portrait works. Is this the same man and woman as in 'it could happen to you'? Does it detail an erotic episode from their past? Is it a memory, or a fantasy, of an assignation with another partner (an unknown man; or the resentful young woman in 'portrait with cigarette' perhaps)? Is the fantasy solely erotic, or does it have darker and more pathological undertones?

Munch's paintings run the gamut of the big existential themes, highlighting the human figure against a backdrop of dread and uncertainty, haunted by the demons of anxiety, sex and death. Products of a turbulent *fin-de-siècle* imagination, these images continue to reverberate with all the power and intensity of archetypes. Wracked by the vicissitudes of love, by premonitions of mortality, by the instabilities and insecurities of identity, the subjects of Anne Katrine Dolven's video portraits inhabit an equally fickle and arbitrary universe. Munch's landmark images hover behind them like ghosts, casting shadows into the present; symbols of angst and foreboding, but also of time-honoured existential truths. Dolven's subjects, though, are very much their own people, embodied in a landscape that is immediately recognisable as our own; a world in which anything can happen to anyone at any given moment, where the emotions that inspire us and the events that overtake us arrive out of nowhere, from out of the blue. In these striking and affecting film and video pieces, Dolven offers a vision as stark and compelling as Munch's original works; less severe perhaps, less ominous, but strangely beguiling, all-too-human.

Anne Katrine Dolven in conversation
with Ele Carpenter

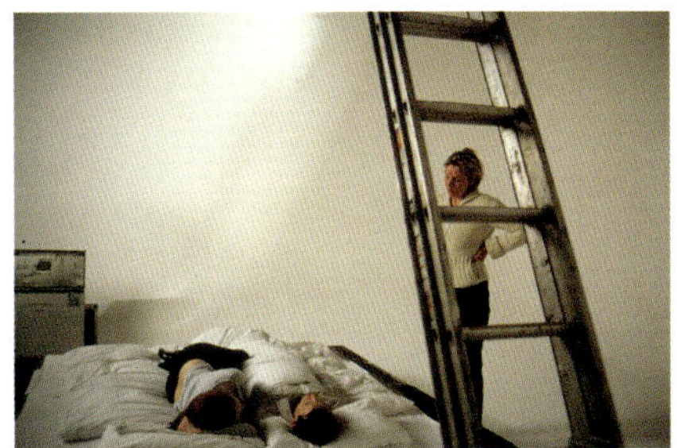

Ele Carpenter You are an artist who works in video and film, and who also continues to make paintings. When you were directing 'it could happen to you', I noticed you spending a lot of time positioning and repositioning objects within the frame of the camera, balancing light, shadow and composition. These are the formal concerns of painting as well as film-making – the bed was a bit like a blank canvas on which you were composing the image. Could you talk more about the differences, and similarities, between making a film and making a painting?

Anne Katrine Dolven Art offers a unique opportunity to focus and go deeper into a subject, but it also allows the artist the freedom to choose what they consider to be the most appropriate medium for a particular work. The basis of all my works is a concept, or, to use a more simple word, a feeling. Some of those feelings translate immediately to film; others are better expressed in painting. What a lot of the works share, however, whether they are shot with a camera, or painted on canvas or aluminium, is a sense of exploring the edge of the frame. The way that I use the frame in video is similar to the way I would use the four sides of a painting. This is not just a formal matter: I am interested in what we 'see' in the work, in *how you touch the edge*, but also in how it touches upon an 'unseen' element, an element of the imagination, which exists outside the frame. Film and video are particularly interesting media for me because of the element of duration, the unexpected things, and also the expected things, that happen over time. With a painting, you have to give yourself time to see. In a film, time is given to you, it is served up in a different way.

Ele Do you feel that you have less control over the process of making a film than a painting?

Anne Katrine Not at all. Things happen with the material no matter what the material is. You can listen to that or suppress it. Previously I used to try to control it, but I think I am more in tune with what happens now, more able to enter into a dialogue with the material. For me, a painting evolves over a different period of time from a film. Painting is also more abstract, it offers other opportunities and involves a different way of thinking. Painting and video are like different languages. Like when you say 'I love you'. Sometimes it works best in words. Sometimes body language is enough. When I begin a painting, the surface of the canvas is a 'nothing', but as soon as you turn on the camera and point it, you immediately have 'something'. I love both these surfaces.

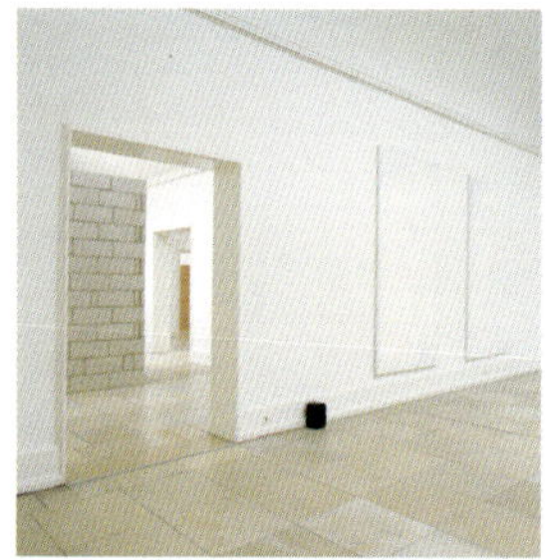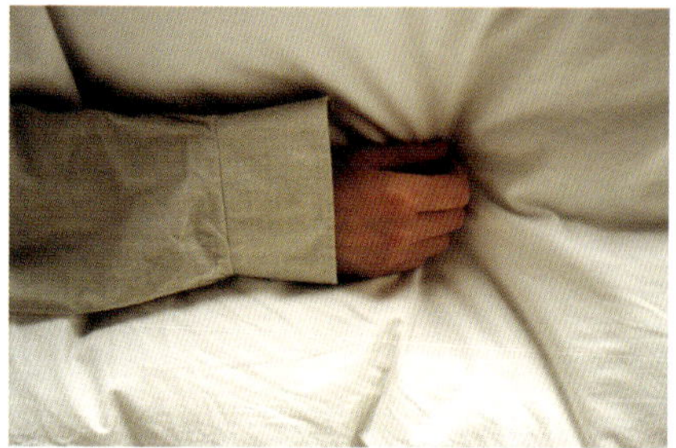

Ele When you are planning a new video or film, how much are theme, narrative and characters developed in your mind before you start?

Anne Katrine I always have a clear idea before I start. Sometimes I use people in my films, but I also use objects, or landscapes where location and light is central. The works that revolve around natural light are often shot in the north of Norway. There the light changes a lot, not only throughout the year, but within the course of a single day, so a shoot has to be well-planned. When I work with people, they are always people I know well, carefully chosen in relation to what I want to highlight in the film. I tried to use an actor once and it didn't work at all. Of course, it takes time to build up the element of trust that is at the heart of this way of working. There has to be trust both ways, a trust in the nature of the relationship that goes on even after the work has been produced. I have a kind of ongoing responsibility to the people I've included in my films, one that makes me particularly sensitive to the way they are portrayed or represented; which again is very different from the temporary relationship I might have working with professional actors.

Ele 'it could happen to you' explores a sensitive, delicate, ambiguous relationship. How did you begin to think about making this work?

Anne Katrine I saw a film when I was very young, in the early 70s, by Ingmar Bergman, called 'Cries and Whispers'. My lasting memory of the film is of a dying woman sitting in her bed. All her family is waiting outside for her to die. Then her childhood nanny comes into the room and goes up to her, in the bed, and offers her breast to comfort the sick woman. It wasn't until many years later that the image came back to me. I had been interested for a while in making a work that describes an end rather than a beginning; not necessarily a death scene as such but a situation where one is exhausted for different reasons. I chose a man and a woman as the subjects, but it could equally have been two women or two men. For me, the choice was natural because of the close relationship between the two people, and the element of trust that exists between them.

I made three works in 2000 ('portrait with cigarette', 'puberty' and 'The Kiss') that clearly relate to specific paintings by Munch. This new film is something else. But it's quite interesting that the motif of the red hair on the pillow also relates back to Munch, and his painting 'The Sick Child'. In the Munch painting,

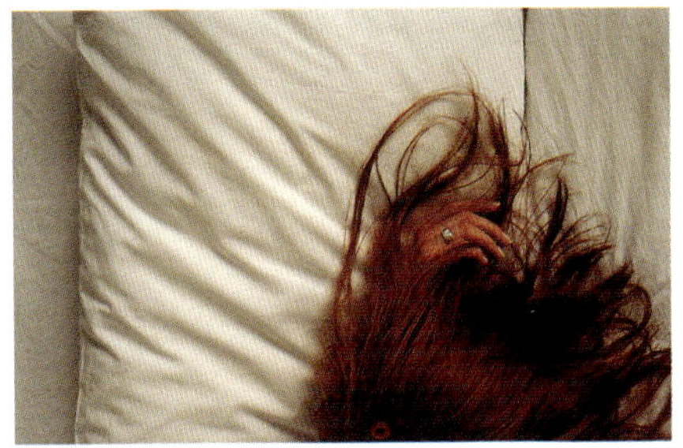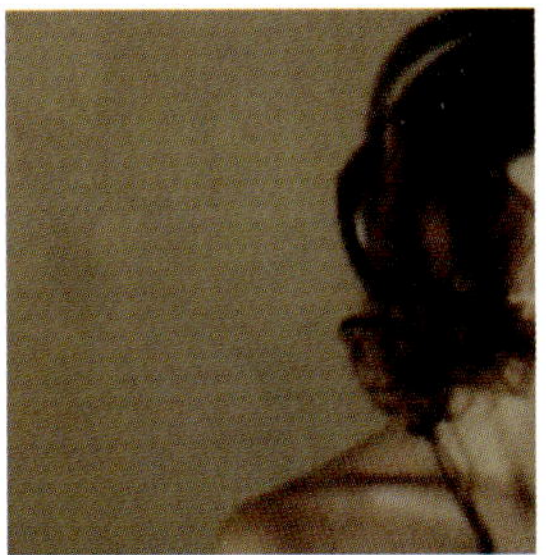

the girl is dying with her head on her pillow, whereas in my film she is full of life. She has her high-heeled boots on, and you can imagine her either coming in from or going out dancing.

'The Sick Child' was an image I found on a postcard at home when I was thirteen. I made a copy in oil paint on a piece of board and gave it to my aunt for Christmas! (She gave it back to me some years ago.) I had never been to the gallery (in Oslo) and seen the painting for real. At that time I was probably not even aware that the gallery existed. I found the postcard, copied the image, just like I used to copy the front page of a magazine we used to get every week. They were all found images. I am a bit surprised to find this coming through in my work now. Many of the things I am dealing with are close to everyday images. Also the music I use is very much a part of everyday contemporary culture.

Ele In the painting, although the child is in bed, it seems that she is comforting the woman sitting at her bedside, which one presumes is her mother or a relative. The comfort is not from the carer to the sick person, but from the sick person to the carer. You have managed to capture some of the ambiguity of this image in your film. How did you communicate what you wanted to achieve to the two protagonists?

Anne Katrine 'it could happen to you' is somehow different from my other films. This film describes a much deeper relationship with something happening between the characters over time. I didn't intend to define the narrative too strongly, preferring to leave this process to the two people themselves. The development of the scene relies entirely on their understanding of what the film is about. It depends upon how they are acting or behaving and the chemistry between them while they are being filmed. We talked a lot about this and did some test filming. The first few times I directed them – talking them through the relationship. Then we agreed not to do this and just let them do it on their own. None of my films have any edits. This one was due to last for four minutes, which is the length of a roll of 35mm film. We used every frame, so in the end the work is four minutes and nine seconds. It is based on lots of trust, on the two people knowing each other very well, and sharing what the idea is about. It is quite different from the other films that consist of one fixed pose. On those, I worked alone in my own studio, or with one or two others. But for this film, which was shot in a film studio on 35mm, there were many more people involved. That team process is new for me. I had a whole team around me doing all the technical work. After a while, I realised I could just focus on directing the film. When the camera was rolling, I was free to watch what was happening, and there were some moving and magical moments.

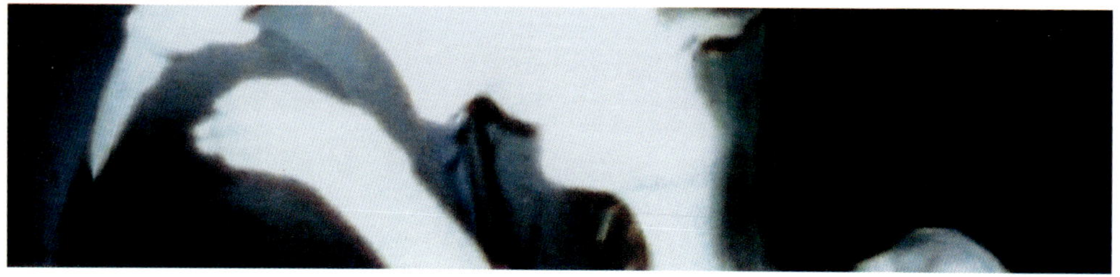

Ele Each time I watch the film I see it and understand it in a different way. It forces you to ask questions and tests your memory and how one makes assumptions about people and relationships without really thinking. I have to re-view it again and again.

Anne Katrine It is a complex work, and there are several ways to see it. It is based on a moment of life, when you are first born and you can't see but you sort of feel with your mouth – you search with your mouth. After that, we go through life and we communicate with other people, explore who we are socially, intellectually, politically and this colours our moves. Here is someone with closed eyes, a grown-up person, and again he is just searching with his mouth. In what kind of stage, or state, is he? We do not know exactly what is happening, but it is an important moment when a lot of our preconceptions are wiped away.

Ele You made a number of works last year about kissing, each piece exploring increasingly more complex and ambiguous relationships. Artists like Munch, Klimt or Rodin usually present a classically romantic kiss, where the relationships appear to be fairly straightforward. There may be hidden layers of ambiguity, but, within the culture of their time, they are read in a very particular way. Your work revives the potential of what a kiss can be, highlighting the complexity of relationships between two people.

Anne Katrine My work 'The Kiss' is a classical image in a contemporary context. The location could be a club, though the piece suggests a very intimate relationship between the couple. The heavy bass beat of the House music is important in situating the time and place of the work. The young woman's red bracelets, which relate to her pulse, are something you could buy in any fashion shop. The red ear of the man is also in the Munch painting, reflecting where the light comes from but also the excitement in the pale face. Very normal.

Ele Romantic love is commonly portrayed in film, used in advertising, magazines and television; and is full of clichés. Many artists may be apprehensive about approaching such a subject because of the danger of falling into these clichés. I wonder how you manage to avoid them?

Anne Katrine We are all busy thinking about issues such as love, but we don't talk about them, at least not when we have passed a certain age or academic level. It is a fine line to tread, and that's why it is exciting to walk it again and again.

Reconstructed Images
Michael Glasmeier

Tableaux vivants are a curious art form. They began in antiquity, acquired great political significance during the pageants of the Renaissance and, finally, in the eighteenth century, were put to the service of the emerging bourgeoisie. In the nineteenth century, *tableaux vivants* became a favourite subject for photographers, who used models to stage scenes from old masters. Bourgeois citizens and artists alike enjoyed having their picture taken, dressed up in costume and striking well-known poses, in order to reconstruct famous paintings by Raphael, Guido Reni or Adriaen Brouwer. We encounter twentieth century versions of such tableaux in the work of photographers such as Duchamp, Man Ray or Sherman, but also in the films of Godard and Jarman; in tapes by Viola and Hill and in performances by Abramovic as well as Fluxus artists and others.

This brief summary must suffice in order to demonstrate that such reconstructed images possess their own, albeit unwritten, history. The reason for this is that *tableaux vivants* took place privately and, prior to the nineteenth century, were only mentioned in literature (Goethe's 'Elective Affinities', for example) if at all. This precluded the genre from being regarded as an independent artistic medium in its own right. Instead, *tableaux vivants* were seen as a form of entertainment: there was pleasure to be had in donning a disguise, not to mention the kudos a connoisseur could acquire at being able to recognise great works of art.

Anne Katrine Dolven's decision to bring to life several of Edvard Munch's masterpieces places her work firmly within the aforementioned tradition. However, her tapes do more than merely embrace this tradition in that they look beyond the genre of *tableaux vivants* to penetrate their particular system. Her video pieces 'puberty', 'portrait with cigarette' and 'The Kiss', all of which were produced last year, create *tableaux vivants* that are active; rather than presenting the viewer with a motionless, statue-like embodiment of a painting, Dolven's tableaux include a rhythm, based on contemporary pop music such as House and techno. Rhythms such as these introduce an element of temporality to a scene which should, ideally, be timeless. Thus, in 'puberty', the naked young woman bobs up and down and, in doing so, loses the sense of existentialist angst which is Munch's subject. The androgynous subject of 'portrait with cigarette' switches between different music channels; here, the artist is not so much portrayed as a thinker but as an active, self-confident presence, who appears to have little concern for such things as health. Finally, in 'The Kiss', the never-ending embrace focuses on the couple's total absorption in the act – which was Munch's intention; although Dolven's use of music makes it abundantly clear that we are observing a couple which belongs very much to this world. The red ear which emerges as the focus of the piece indicates the 'hearing' of another age which is both parallel and contemporary.

In this way, Anne Katrine Dolven transcends Edvard Munch's existentialist speechlessness. In Dolven's work, the suffering of one Nordic artist is transposed by another Nordic artist to an age in which self-definition and the search for identity are closely related to the ubiquitousness of public sounds. Dolven amalgamates a once-insular medium with the very public aesthetic experience of music videos and the acoustic avant-garde; in doing so, she ejects an enlightened middle-class from the seclusion of eighteenth century *tableaux vivants*. Thanks to Dolven, the *tableau vivant*, or living image, is released from its historical paradox and comes to life.

In his painting 'The Scream' (1893), Edvard Munch himself tried to create an aggressive sound for the introverted subjects at the heart of his work. This image remains a confusing exception, a less-than-ideal solution to the rest of Munch's *oeuvre*. In his photographs, Munch appears with his models in reconstructed images that are a reference to *tableaux vivants*. Yet here, Munch's use of double-exposure and blurring creates a vital energy that allows one to banish all thought of the ornamental stasis of his painting.

Anne Katrine Dolven takes precisely this juncture as her starting point. She moves her images so that we, the viewers, can be moved by them. In doing so, she demonstrates the vitality of Aby Warburg's *Pathosformeln* (pathos formulae) for our own age. In her *tableaux vivants*, the expressionist passion for the private is transformed into a cool portrait of public identity engaged in a search for self, a search characterised by poses and the *basso continuo* of music.

Translated from the German by Lindsey Merrison

it could happen to you 2001
35mm film as projection, 4' 9", edition of 5, plus A/P
Camera: Martin Testar; Lighting: Danny Murphy; Production Co-ordinator: Bevis Bowden
Filmed at Holborn Studios, London
Commissioned by Film and Video Umbrella and Northern Gallery for Contemporary Art

portrait with cigarette 2000
Video on 3:4 flat screen, 6' 18", edition of 3, plus A/P
Speakers on opposite wall
Camera and lighting: Alexandra Henao; Editor: Richard Horn at The Lux, London
Filmed at The Tannery, London

puberty 2000
Video projection, 5' 29", edition of 3, plus A/P
Camera and lighting: Alexandra Henao; Editor: Richard Horn at The Lux, London
Filmed at The Tannery, London

The Kiss 2000
16mm film, 7' 44", edition of 5, plus A/P
Presented as a video projection in a Yton/brick house. Sound from sub woofer
Camera and lighting: Alexandra Henao; Editors: Richard Horn at the Lux, London
and Tariq Sheik at MTV, London
Filmed at The Tannery, London

headlights 2001
Video on 9:16 flat screen, 6', edition of 5, plus A/P
Camera: Vegar Moen; Editor: Richard Horn at Team Pictures Ltd, London
Filmed at Stolpestad, Hedmark, Norway

Courtesy carlier | gebauer, Berlin and Anthony Wilkinson Gallery, London; portrait with cigarette and puberty courtesy carlier | gebauer, Berlin

it could happen to you
2001

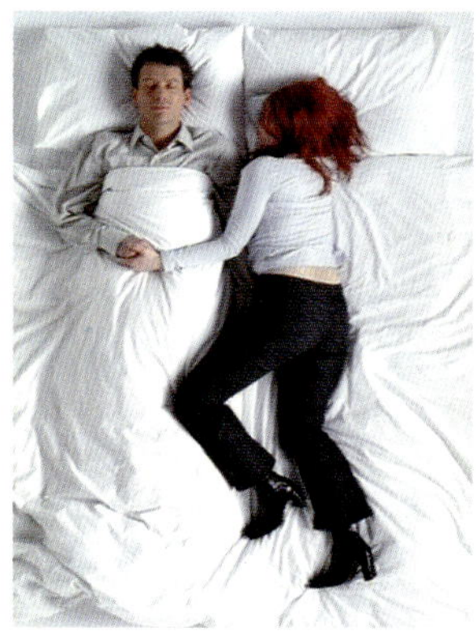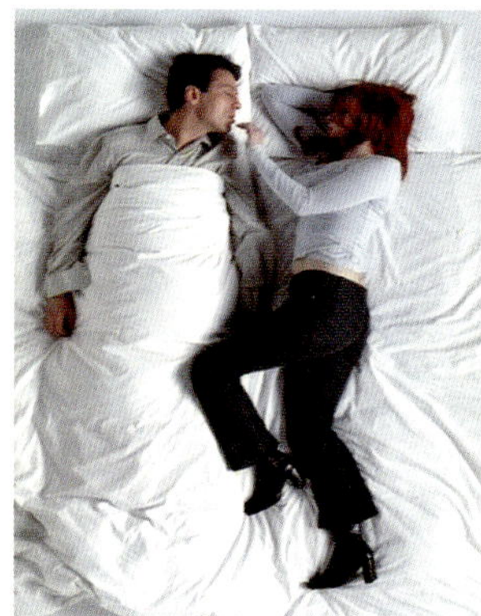

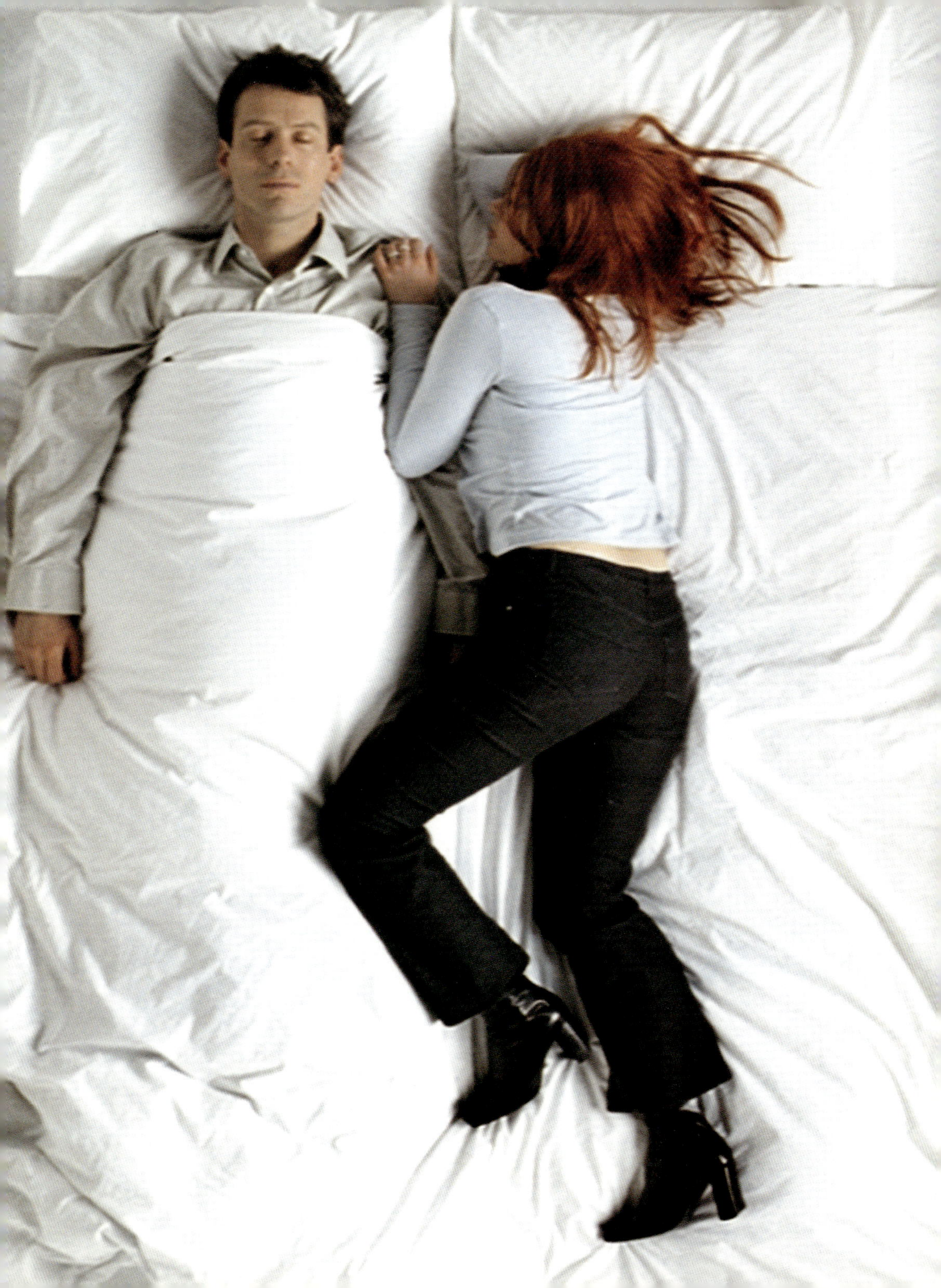

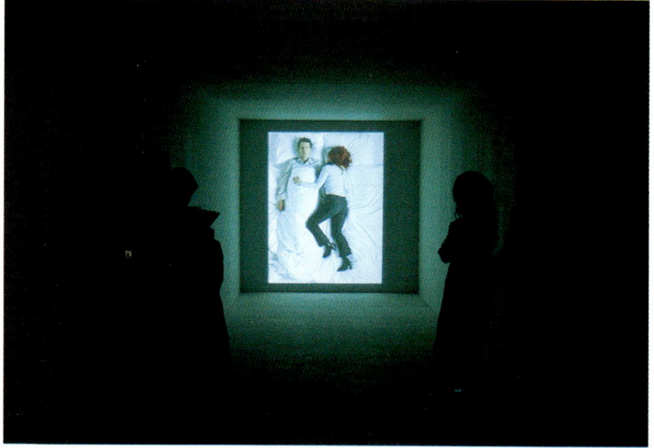

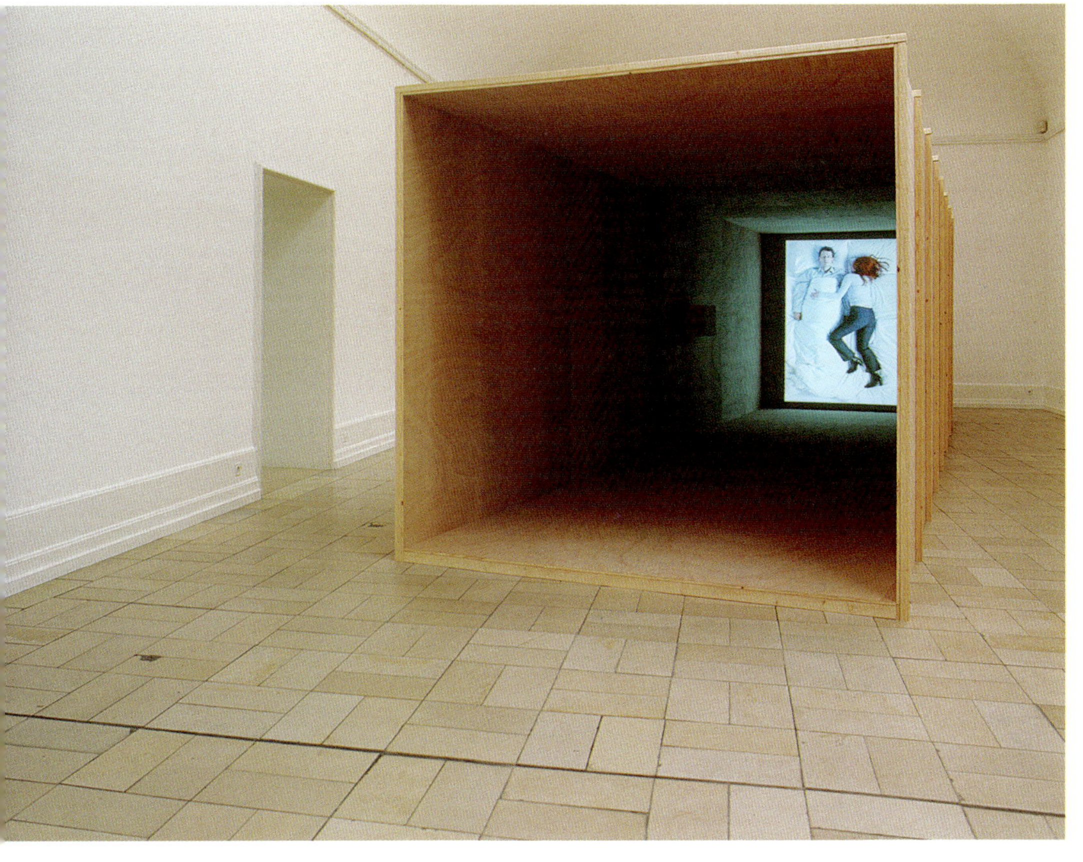

portrait with cigarette
2000

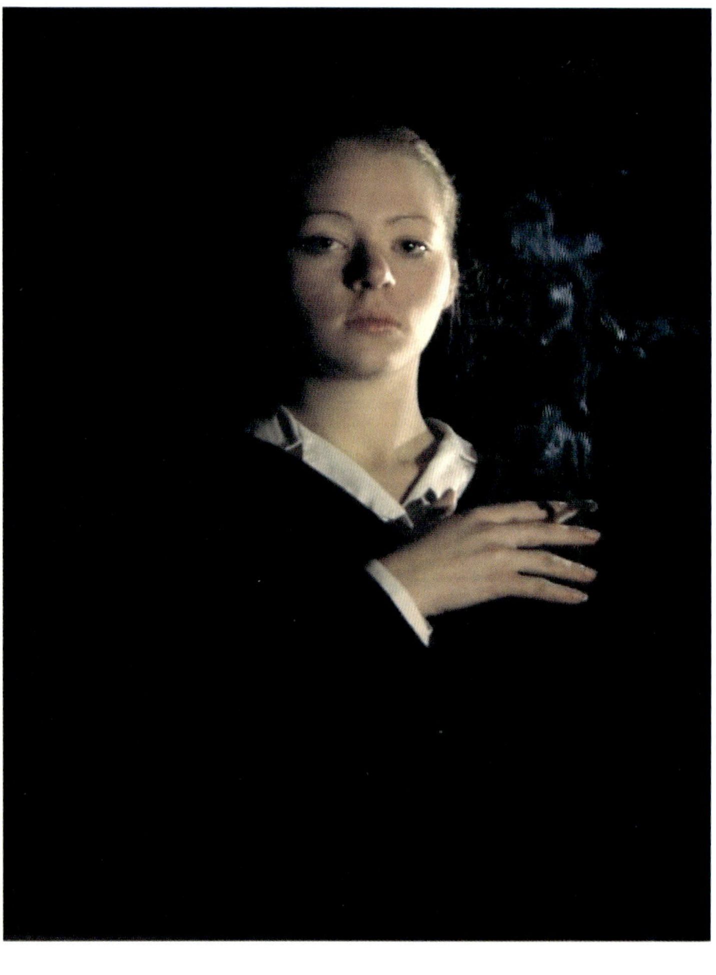

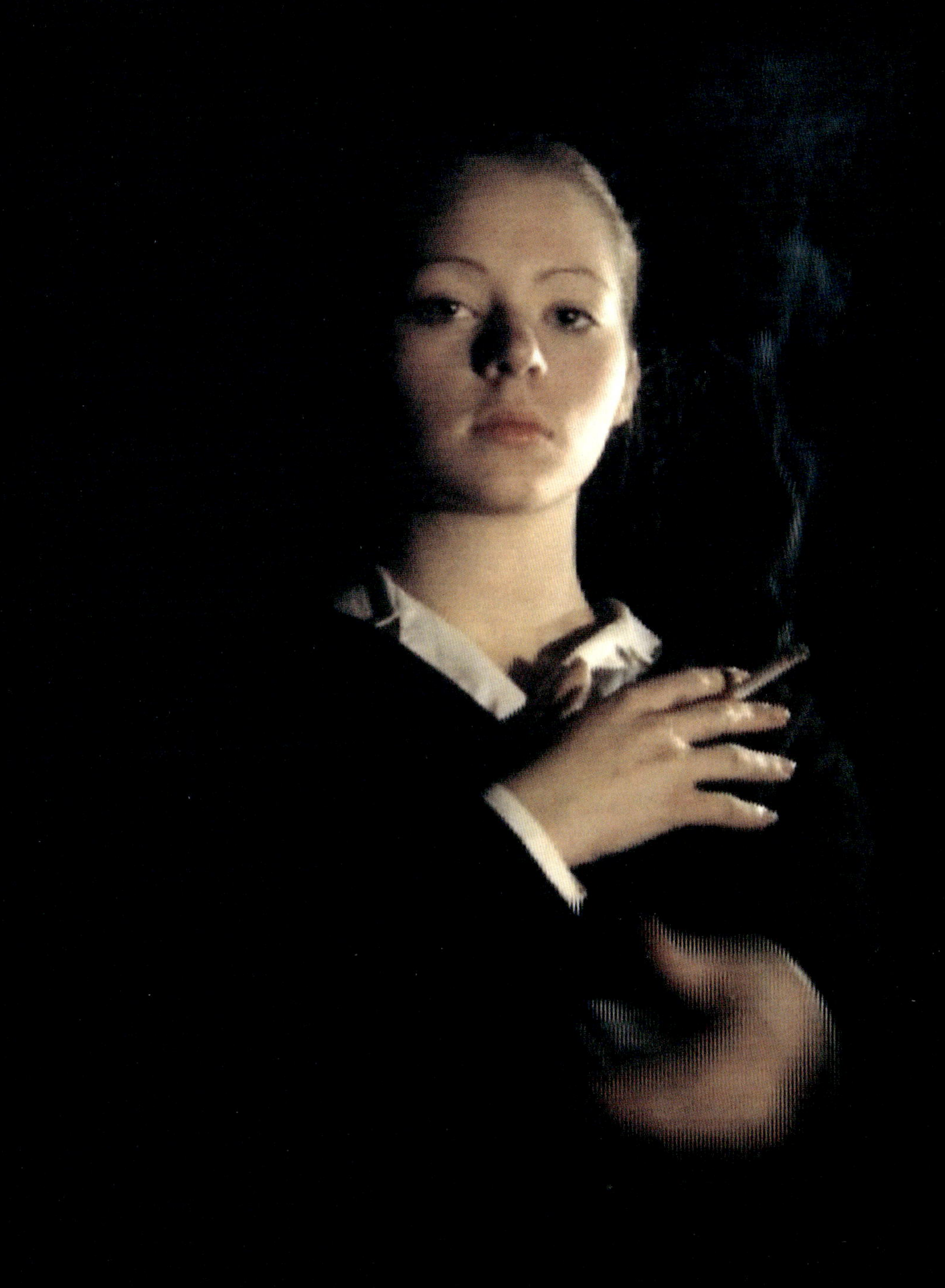

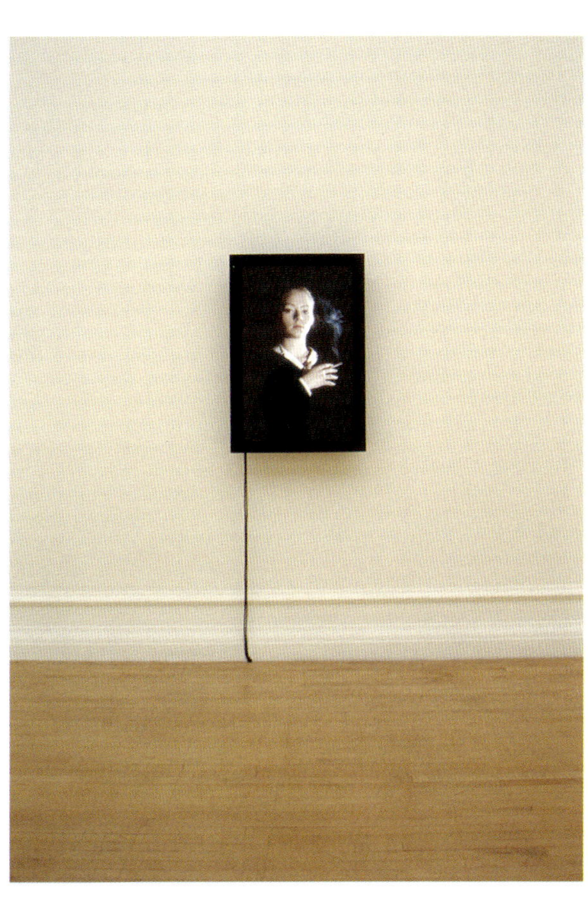

puberty

2000

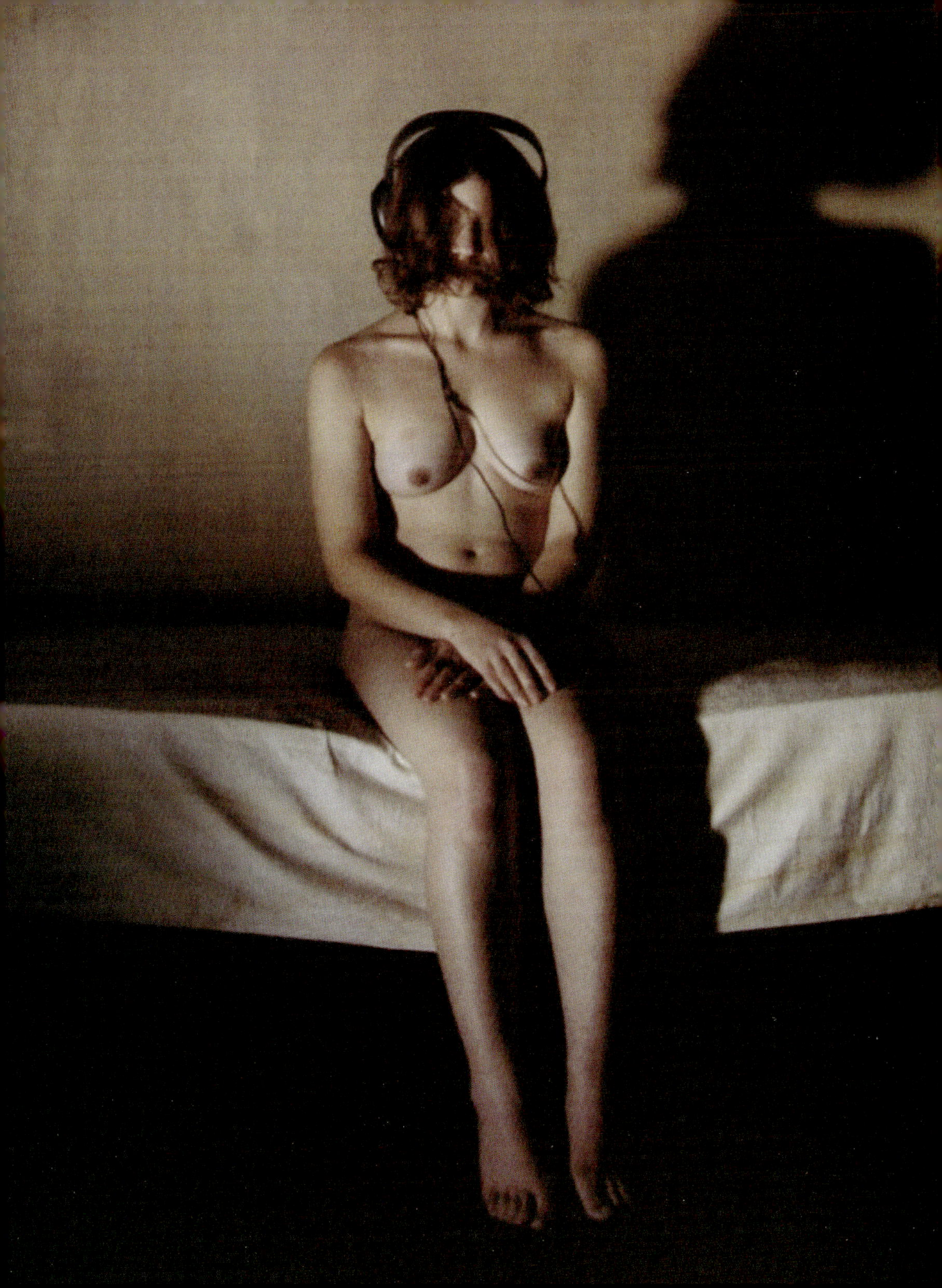

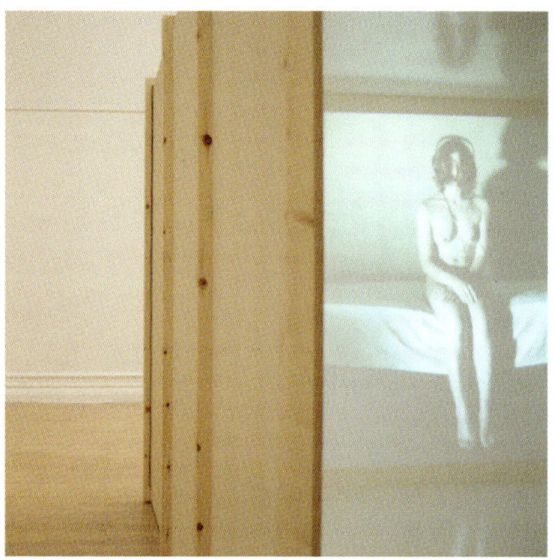

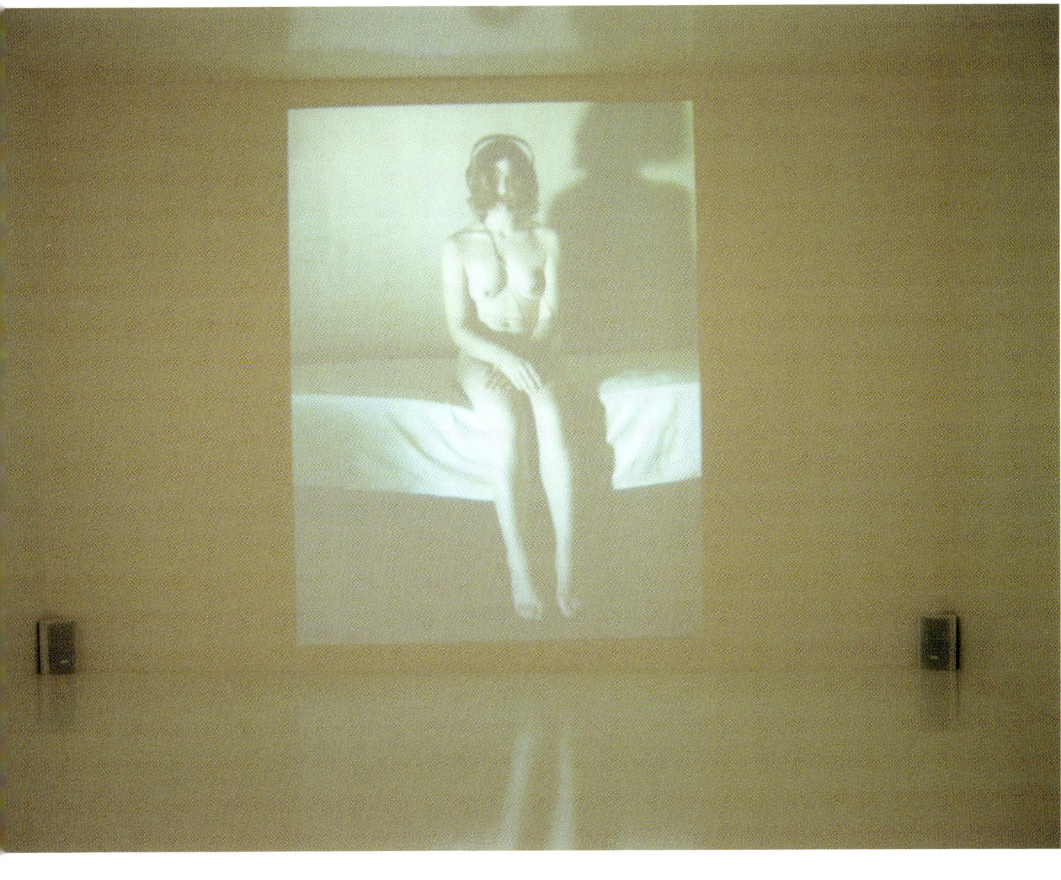

The Kiss

2000

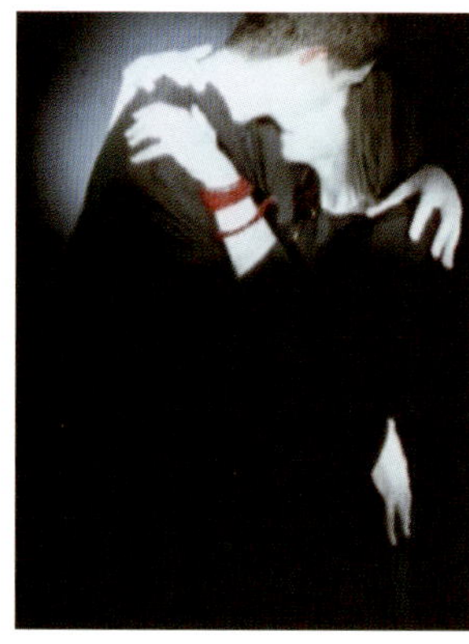 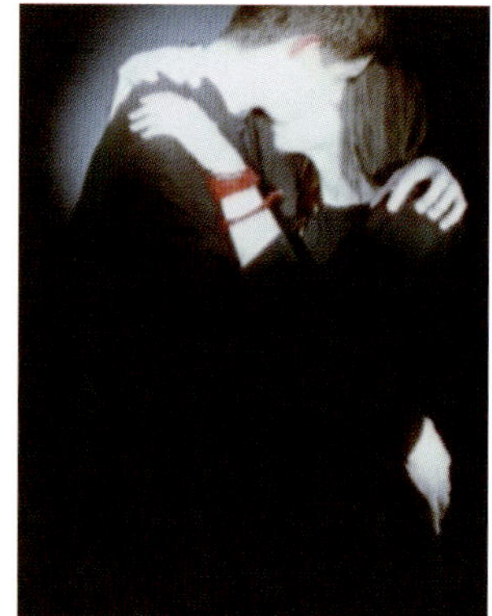

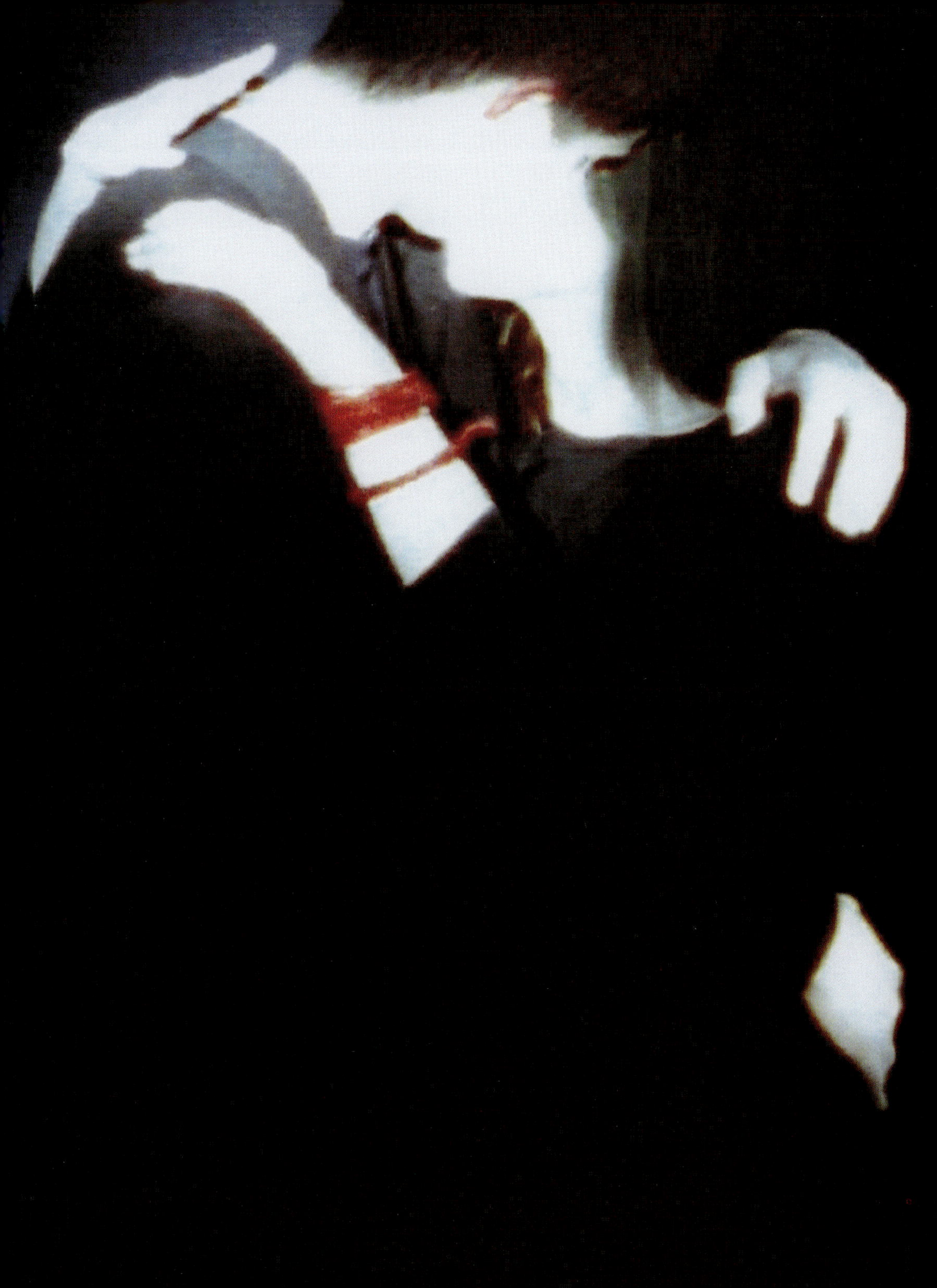

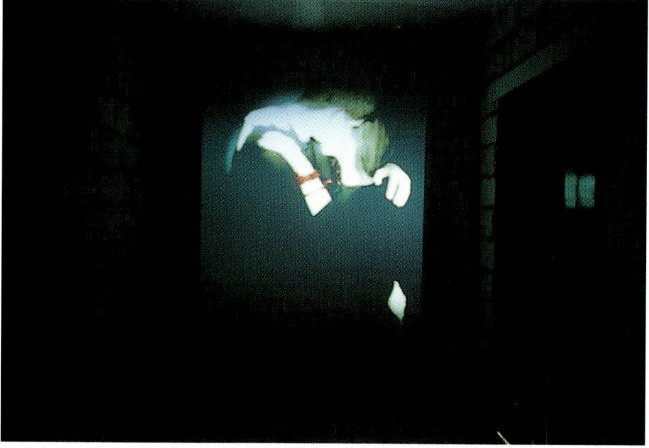

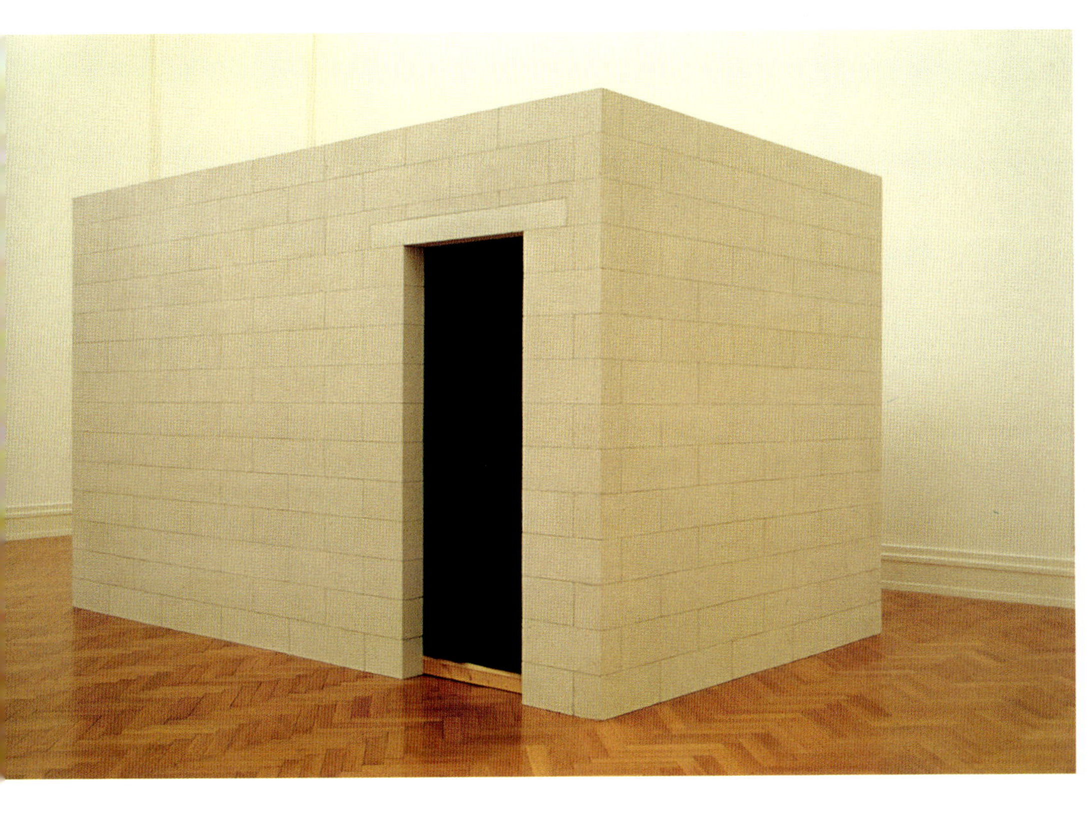

headlights

2001

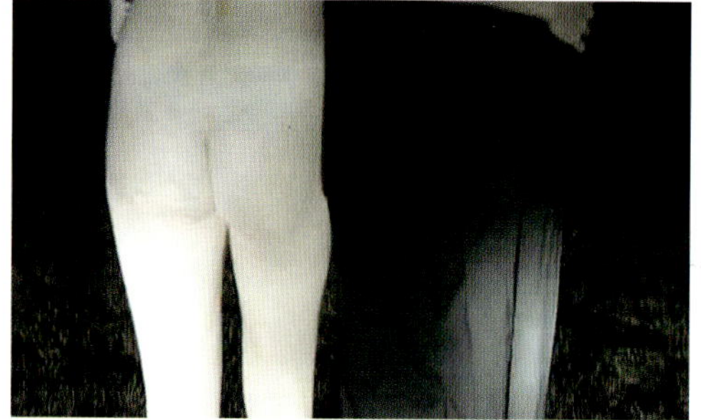

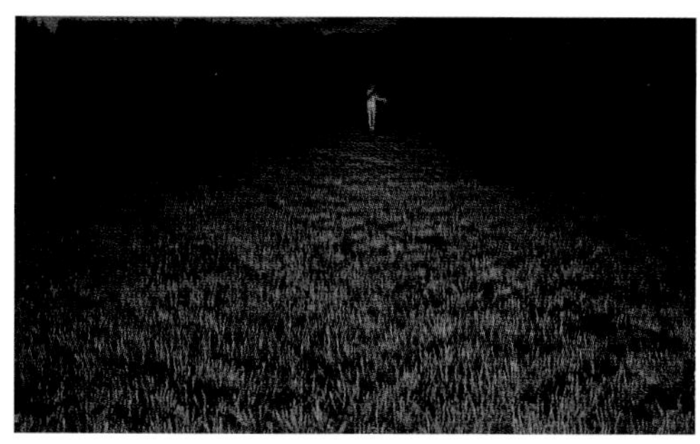

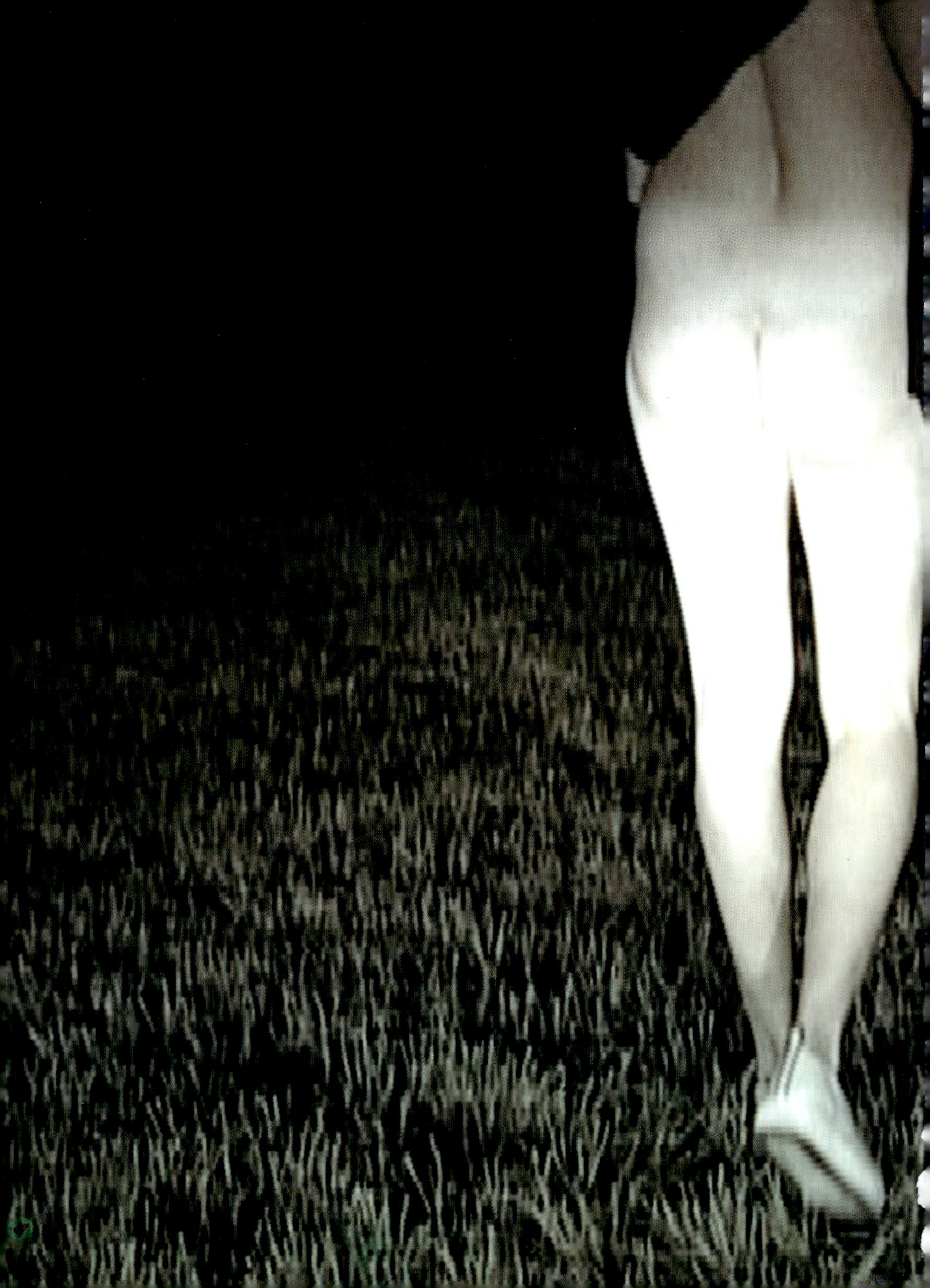

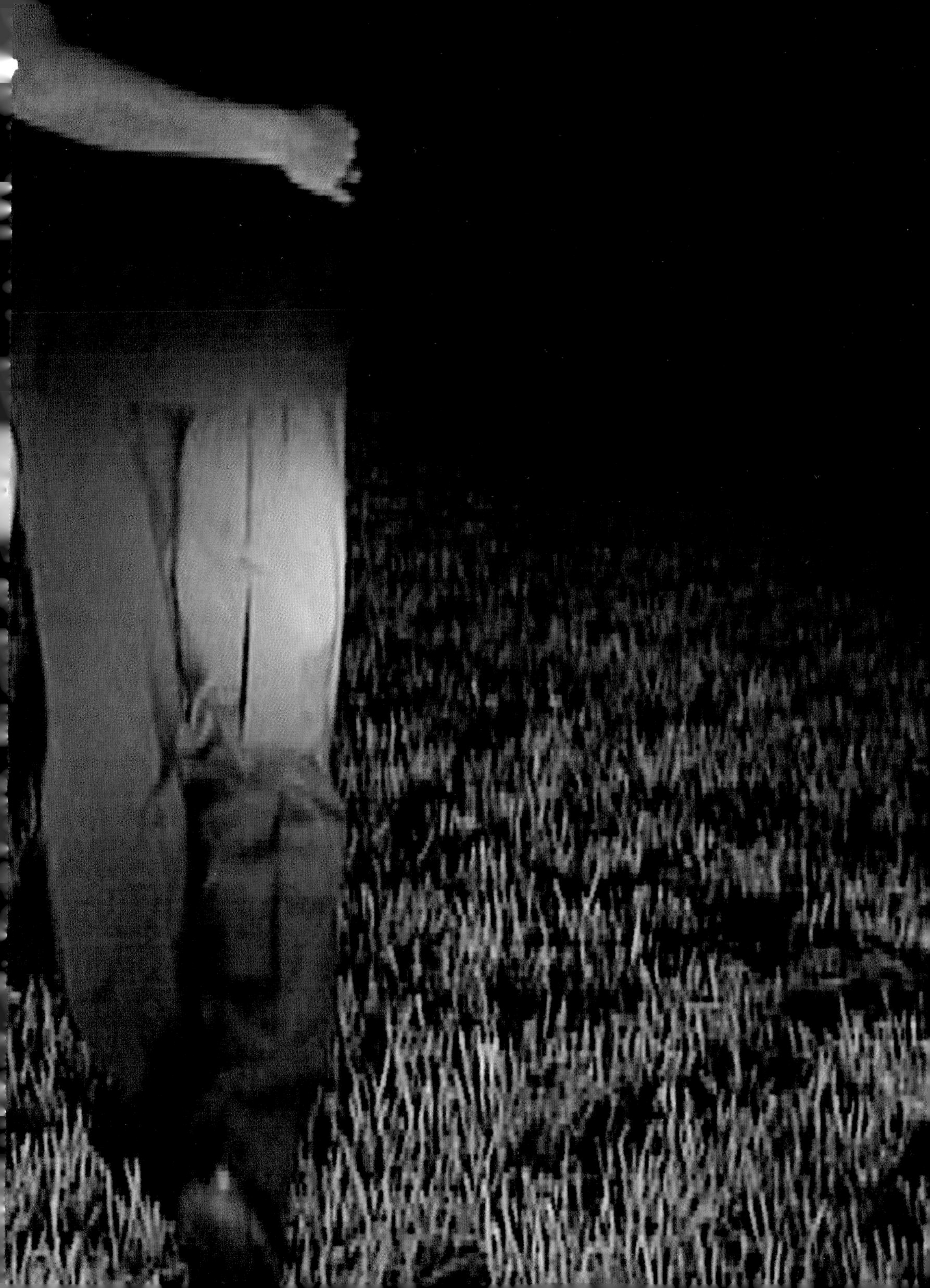

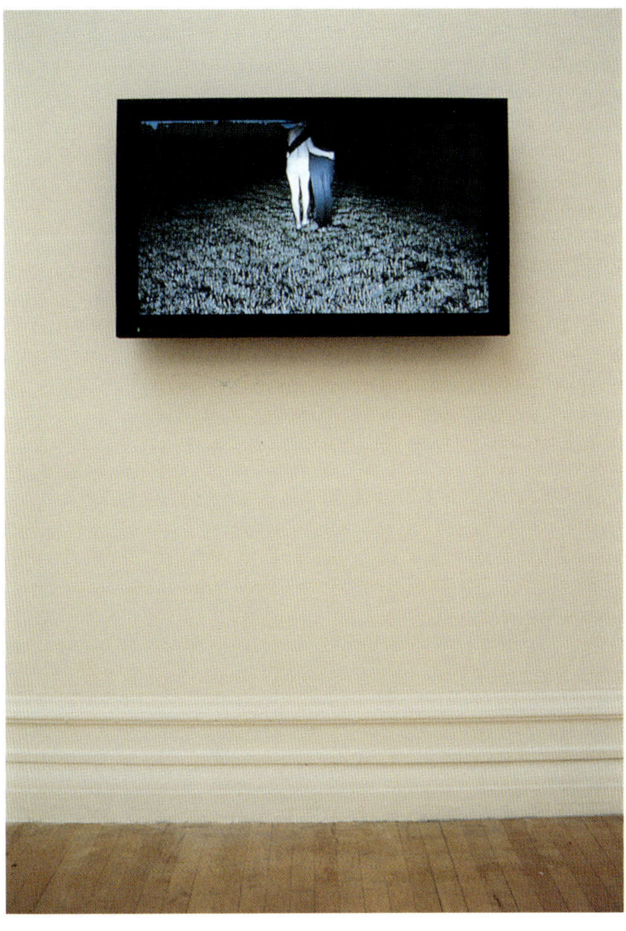

A K Dolven
Born in Oslo, Norway
Lives in Lofoten and London

Solo Exhibitions (selected)

2002
Henie Onstad Kunstsenter, Oslo*
carlier | gebauer, Berlin

2001
Site Gallery, Sheffield
South London Gallery, London*
Kunsthalle Bern*
Gallery Bouhlou, Bergen
Northern Gallery for Contemporary Art, Sunderland
Kunsthalle Nürnberg*
Visual Art at Sadlers Wells, Sadlers Wells, London
In residence, Kunstnernes Hus, Oslo*
Videos and Films 1995-2001, Moderna Museet, Stockholm

2000
Anthony Wilkinson Gallery, London
Galerie Gebauer, Berlin
13 Quai Voltaire, Caisse des Depots, Paris
Fred Thieler Prize in Painting, Berlinische Galerie, Berlin*
Galleri i8, Reykjavik

1999
Video Gallery, Philadelphia Museum of Art, Philadelphia

1998
Special Someone, Galerie Gebauer, Berlin
Januar, Gallery ANHAVA, Helsinki
Artist of the Year, Norwegian International Filmfestival,
Haugesund Billedgalleri, Norway
Galleri Bouhlou, Bergen

1997
The Power of the Flower, Galleri 29, Växjö, Sweden

1996
short happiness last long, Galerie Gebauer u. Thumm, Berlin*
teenagers and balconies, Galleri STRUTS, Oslo*

1995
Galleri Bouhlou, Bergen*
til deg, Bodø Kunstforening, Bodø, Norway*

1994
drop me drop you, Gallery ANHAVA, Helsinki*
Tromsø Kunstforening, Tromsø, Norway
starting over, Galerie Gebauer u. Günther, Berlin*
to you, permanent outdoor sculpture, Hå, Norway and Munich*

1993-1997
engel, permanent outdoor sculpture in Oslo, Lodz, Berlin and Derry*

1992
linkshändig engel rechtshändig engel, Galerie Gebauer u. Günther,
Berlin*
Gallery Adelgatan 5, Malmö
Henie Onstad Kunstsenter, Oslo*

1991
1991, Nordic Art Center, Helsinki*
Bergen Kunstforening

1990
Thorden Gallery, Gothenburg
Galleri 29, Växjö, Sweden

1988
Künstlerhaus Bethanien, Berlin*
Artist of the Year, Nord Norske Festspill, Harstad, Norway*
Wang Galleri, Oslo*

*denotes exhibition catalogue or cards/posters made by the artist

Group Exhibitions (selected)

2002
Moving Portraits, Wood Street Galleries, Pittsburgh, PA. (Luc
Courchesne, Bea De Visser, A K Dolven, Bill Viola, Gillian Wearing)*

2001
Impulser, H.M. The Queen's Collection, Henie Onstad Kunstsenter, Oslo*
Mouvement Immobiles, Museum of Contemporary Art, Buenos Aires
(Vanessa Beecroft, Dino Bruzzone, Jordi Colomer, Tacita Dean,
A K Dolven, Philippe Durand, Claudia Fontes, Marine Hugonnier,
Pierre Joseph, Jorge Macchi, Philippe Parreno, Ugo Rondinone,
Franck Scurti, Alessandra Tesi, Gabriel Valansi)*
Objects In A Mirror Are Closer Than They Appear, TEAM Gallery,
New York (Janet Biggs, Rebecca Bournigault, Slater Bradley,
Olaf Breuning, A K Dolven, Maria Friberg, Maria Marshall)
Moving Pictures, Villa Merkel, 5th International Foto Triennale,
Esslingen, Germany (Kolpa Abda, A K Dolven, Stan Douglas,
Kathrin Gunther, Douglas Gordon, Sharon Lockhart, Aernout Mik,
Cindy Sherman, Anne Schneider, Grgor Zapp)*
My Friends, Tromsø Kunstforening, Tromsø, Norway (Kjetil Berge,
Tacita Dean, A K Dolven, Matthew Hale)*
On the Way to the Screen: Video of the 90s, Central House of Artists,
Moscow (Eija-Liisa Ahtila, A K Dolven, Graham Gussin, Soo Ja Kim,
Shirin Neshat, Pierrick Sorin, Jaan Toomik)
Humid, Spike Island, Bristol and Melbourne Festival, Australia
(Christine Borland, Kate Daw, Tacita Dean, A K Dolven,
Mariele Neudecker, Pipilotti Rist, Nina Saunders)
Lens and Paper/The Beauty of Intimacy, Gemeentemuseum den
Haag, Kunsthalle Baden Baden, Haus am Waldsee, Berlin*

2000
Century of Innocence, Rooseum, Malmö*
sensitive, le printemps de Cahors, Cahors, France*
Paintings, Bomuldsfabriken, Arendal, Norway
Nordic Postmodernism, KIASMA, Helsinki
The Other Side of Zero, Tate, Liverpool (A K Dolven,
Dryden Goodwin, Monika Oechsler)*
BRUCE DE CAMINAS, Artists from Berlin, Sala Plaza de Espana
de la Comunidad, Madrid*
Shelter, Trondheim Kunstforening*
Waterfront, Helsingborg, Sweden*
Carnegie Art Award for Nordic Painting, Barbican, London*
Collection from the 90s, Museum of Contemporary Art, Oslo

1999
The 6th International Istanbul Biennial, Istanbul,*
Intercourse, Toronto (A K Dolven, John Nixon, Ann Schneider)
ninenineninetynine, Anthony Wilkinson Gallery, London
BLICK – Film and Video, Moderna Museet, Stockholm
The Waters, Orchard Gallery, Derry, N. Ireland (Dorothy Cross,
A K Dolven, Tacita Dean, Marie Jo Lafontaine, Nigel Rolfe)
Eksenter, Våganhallen, Svolvær, Norway* (Johnny Björnebakk,
A K Dolven, Geir Tore Holm, Esko Männikö, Mikkel McAlinden, N55,
Ole Jörgen Ness, Spencer Tunick, Magnus Wallin, Gillian Wearing)
Carnegie Art Award, Kunstnernes Hus, Oslo*

1998
Fellessentralen, Kunstnernes Hus, Oslo*
Videoforum, Art Forum, Berlin
MOMENTUM, Nordic Festival of Contemporary Art, Moss, Norway*
Pictures for the Blue Room, A Contemporary Art Exhibition in the
Vigeland Museum, Oslo*

1997
Summer of Love, Fotouhi Cramer Gallery, New York
Norske Profiler, Museum Folkwang, Essen, Rostock Kunsthalle, Germany*
Screens: International Video, Trondheim Kunstforening, Trondheim
Virtual Gallery, project with Oil of Ulay, ITV and Institute of
Contemporary Arts, London (A K Dolven, Tracey Emin, Leila Galloway,
Nina Saunders, Pat Whiteread)

1996
Strangers in the Arctic, Rundetårn, Copenhagen, Museum of
Contemporary Art, Helsinki, Art Gallery of Ontario, Toronto* (Afrika,
A K Dolven, Ilya Kabakov & Pavel Pepperstein, Per Kirkeby, Jussi Kivi,
Ian McKeever, Esko Männikö & Pekka Turunen, Richard Prince,
Ulf Rollof, Maura Sheehan, Georg Steinmann)
Heimat, Kunsthaus Kaufbeuren, Kaufbeuren, Germany*
Eine Vitrine, Helsinki Art Hall, Helsinki* (Christian Boltanski. A K Dolven,
Marcel Broothaers, Hans-Peter Feldmann, Paul-Arman Gette, Inge Mahn,
Annette Messager, Ann Noel/Emmet Willaims, Herman Pitz)
Comp in Box, Galerie ANHAVA, Helsinki
Kunst im Kasten, Berlinische Galerie, Museum for Modern Art
and Photography, Berlin
Neben den Linden, Düsseldorf Kunstverein

1995
Bild und Malerie, Galerie Wohnmaschine, Berlin*

ALLÉGORIE DE LA RICHESSE, Baroque et art contemporain, Chapelle
St. Louis de la Sâlpetrière, Paris (Elisabeth Ballet, Daniel Buren,
A K Dolven, Roland Eckelt, Svetlana Kopystiansky, Johan Lorbeer,
Inge Mahn, Eliseo Mattiacci, Marcel Odenbach, Gundula Schulze,
Jacques Vielle)
Port of Art, Kotka, Finland

1994
Europa 94, Munich*
erzählen, Akademie der Künste, Berlin and Malmö Museum*
(Ayse Erkmen, A K Dolven, Margareta Dreher, Ulrike Grossarth,
Christina Kubisch, Inge Mahn, Simone Mangos, Katharina Meldner,
Helga Paris, Eva-Marie Schön, Gundula Schulze)

1993
5 Bilder, Galerie Gebauer u. Günther, Berlin (Ian Davenport,
A K Dolven, Helmut Federle, Imi Knoebl, Jussi Niva)
interVIEW, Artist Museum, Lodz, Poland*
Winterland, Olympic Exhibition, Atlanta, Tokyo, Munich, Barcelona,
Lillehammer City Museum, Lillehammer, Norway*

1991
Face to Face, Kiel Kunsthalle, Kiel, Germany*
Riga Art Hall, Riga, Latvia

1990
JETZ BERLIN, Malmö Art Hall (A K Dolven, Thomas Florschutz,
Else Gabriel, Bente Geving, Hans Hemmert, Axel Lieber, Sissel Tolaas,
Achim Zeman, Simone Mangos, Georg Zey)

1989
Sangen om Norge, Henie Onstad Kunstsenter, Oslo*

1988
Det grönne mörke, arr. Nordic Art Center, Helsinki* (A K Dolven,
Erik Annar Evensen, Olav Christopher Jenssen, Björn Sigurd Tufta,
Jon Arne Mogstad)

1986
Borealis, DAAD Galerie, Berlin* (A K Dolven, Olav Christopher Jenssen,
Björn Sigurd Tufta, Yngve Zakkarias)

*denotes exhibition catalogue or accompanying publication

Collections

Philadelphia Museum of Art
Berlinische Galerie, Museum of Modern Art and Photography
KIASMA/Museum of Contemporary Art, Helsinki
Arts Council Collection, Great Britain
The National Gallery, Norway
Statens Konstråd, Sweden
Riksgalleriet, Norway
Museum of Contemporary Art, Oslo
Oslo Kommune Art Collection,
Nordland County Art Collection, Norway
Tromsø Museum
Horsens Museum, Denmark
Malmö Museum
Kuperstichkabinett, Berlin
Leipzig Collection of Contemporary Galleries
Hoffmann Collection, Berlin
Städtische Galerie, Wolfsburg
Kunsthalle Bern
H.M. The Queen's Collection, Norway
Private collections

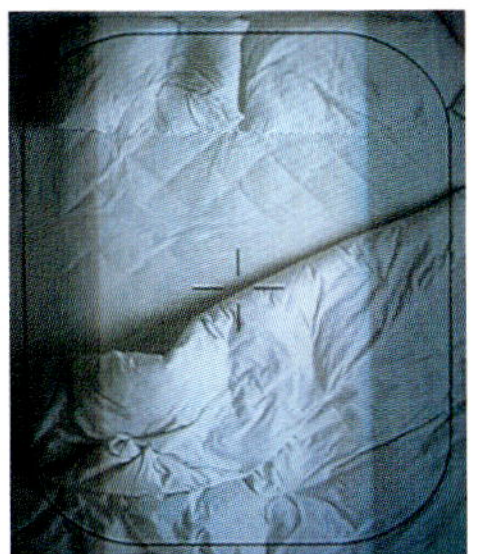

in memory of Olaf

the artist would like to thank

Friends and family, as actors and for all their help.
Kjetil Berge, Lily Wynne-Jones, Sam Phillips, Thora Dolven Balke,
Kristin Jevne, Carl Omsted, Aase Julie Arnkværn, Per Dolven,
Karin Dolven. Steven Bode, Mike Jones, Bevis Bowden, Keith Whittle
and Caroline Smith at Film and Video Umbrella; Ele Carpenter,
Dean Turnbull and Joanna Rowlands at Northern Gallery for
Contemporary Art, Sunderland; Donna Lynas, Margot Heller and
John Mason at South London Gallery; Ellen Seifermann at Kunsthalle
Nürnberg; Bernhard Fibicher at Kunsthalle Bern; Øyvind Stokke
at the Royal Norwegian Embassy, London; Jake Curtin for digital
images; Team Pictures Ltd, London; Vegar Moen; Alexandra Henao.
carlier | gebauer, Berlin; Anthony Wilkinson Gallery, London; Gallery
Bouhlou, Bergen; Gallery ANHAVA, Helsinki, Hitachi Home
Electronics Europe.

This book was published to accompany the film 'it could happen
to you', commissioned by Film and Video Umbrella and Northern
Gallery for Contemporary Art and staged at NGCA in June/July 2001.
This publication was funded by the National Touring Programme
of the Arts Council of England. With additional support from the
Norwegian Ministry for Foreign Affairs, carlier | gebauer, Berlin
and Anthony Wilkinson Gallery, London.

Published in an edition of 1,000
ISBN 0-9538634-5-X
© Film and Video Umbrella, the artist and the authors

Design – Richard Bonner-Morgan
Photography – South London Gallery and 'it could happen to you'
production stills: Bevis Bowden; Kunsthalle Bern: the artist;
Kunsthalle Nürnberg and last page: Annette Kradisch
Printing – Trichrom Limited

film and video umbrella

NORTHERN GALLERY FOR
CONTEMPORARY ART

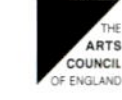

THE
ARTS
COUNCIL
OF ENGLAND